FIRESIDE SERIES

Ramtha

Awakening To The Extraordinary

AWAKENING TO THE EXTRAORDINARY
New Edition

Copyright © 2007 JZ Knight

Cover design by Steve Handlan

ISBN # 1-57873-061-9

JZK Publishing
A Division of JZK, Inc.

RAMTHA'S SCHOOL OF ENLIGHTENMENT
P.O. Box 1210
Yelm, Washington 98597
360.458.5201
800.347.0439
www.ramtha.com
www.jzkpublishing.com

These series of teachings are designed for all the students of the Great Work who love the teachings of the Ram.

It is suggested that you create an ideal learning environment for study and contemplation.

Light your fireplace and get cozy. Prepare yourself. Open your mind to learn and be genius.

FOREWORD

The Fireside Series is an ongoing library of the hottest topics of interest taught by Ramtha. These series of teachings are designed for all the students of the Great Work who love the teachings of the Ram. This collection is also intended as a continuing learning tool for the students of Ramtha's School of Enlightenment and for everyone interested and familiar with Ramtha's teachings. In the last three decades Ramtha has continuously and methodically deepened and expanded his exposition of the nature of reality and its practical application through various disciplines. It is assumed by the publisher that the reader has attended a Beginning Retreat or workshop through Ramtha's School of Enlightenment or is at least familiar with Ramtha's instruction to his beginning class of students. This introductory information is found in *Ramtha: A Beginner's Guide to Creating Reality*, Third Ed. (Yelm: JZK Publishing, a division of JZK, Inc., 2004).

We have included in the Fireside Series a glossary of some of the basic concepts used by Ramtha so the reader can become familiarized with these teachings. We have also included a brief introduction of Ramtha by JZ Knight that describes how all this began for those who are unfamiliar with the story. Enjoy your learning and contemplation.

CONTENTS

WHATSOEVER YOU THINK BECOMES YOUR LIFE

O my beloved God,
of that which you are,
the fire that you be,
Mysterious One,
engage my mind
and move my soul,
expand my consciousness
and evolve my life,
for these days labor I
in that which you are.
God bless my life.
So be it.
To life.

When is living the same boring existence enough? When will you wake up and create a new dream and indeed a new paradigm? In my lifetime I would term those adventures. When you wake up and decide you wish to have an adventure, the ways and means to that adventure simply fall into place because you want it and you are ready for it. It is quite amazing. This is a divine quality and is not coincidence. Consciousness and energy creates the nature of reality, and whatsoever you think becomes your life. It is what gives you that essence of divinity.

It would not be logical or reasonable for you not to use what you were taught. If you do not apply consciously what I have taught you, you can never realize your inheritance fully. The inheritance is that which we call the kingdom of heaven. It has nothing to do with a piece of real estate out there called heaven. It is the ability to transform and indeed transmute matter and time for the purpose of making known the unknown: create, experience, dissolve it, and create again. That is a godlike quality, and we would also call that growth.

You must know it is not enough to simply understand that which is termed philosophy and theory. That is not enough. You have to learn to bring about and give birth to all that is latent in you, and there is a lot that is latent in you. If less than a tenth of your brain has been used this entire lifetime, then what is happening to the rest of it? Why is it still there, and why has it not deformed itself in evolution to be the size of a pea? Have we kept this large brain for the sake of a face? Imagine what your face would look like on a pea. This stands as a mute testament to you and so is the regeneration of lifetimes. There is more for you to do, not in the sense of bigger labor but in the sense of adventure and that which is termed discovery. You have all of the equipment and tools to bring about that manifested kingdom. Life is for experience, to prove that evolutionary factor and manifest that divineness every day.

A master does not let the day happen. The master creates the day and guides it into experience. Truth is taking the knowledge, the philosophy, and then applying it. Little by little you apply the teachings when you are happy because they are easy to apply, and it seems as if God has rained down upon you its most exquisite blessing and that nothing could go wrong. Then one day it does go wrong because you forgot to create that day, so you became subject to reality instead of being its administrator. Then when it goes wrong, you live in the wrong and you become entrenched in a problematic existence. That is where depression comes from, and it becomes a habit. If you are depressed one day, then that sets the standard of existence the next day. You wake up and the next day is rather gloomy because it was given birth by the day before. Then you live the gloom and only foster more of it for the next day. That is its cycle.

There is no reason why any cut on your finger cannot be healed in moments. There is no reason why you should have to beg or worry for your daily bread or your existence because you have learned how to change that. There is no reason for you to have to languor in that which is termed depression, because you have experienced great joy, and it is only the re-remembering of how that came about that would change reality. There is no reason why you have to suffer. Moreover, there is no reason why you should stay stagnated in your boring existence. There is no reason why your life should be mundane, but there is every reason why it should be changing every day.

Change doesn't mean going and kicking the cat out. It is a shift in consciousness that brings a different hue to the day. The light shines differently and casts a different shadow, and the observation of the shadow gives dimensional perspective to the Observer, which is you. It is growth happening every day of your life. There is no reason why you should be at war with your neighbors, and indeed there is no reason why you shouldn't love. If you are God, then you are all. If you have accomplished all that I have taught you forthrightly and experienced it, then God is not a mystery. God is you.

The Box and Free Space

We are going to study the box of the personality in order for you to understand something about the nature of your thinking, how you get stuck in it, and where you give up. How hard must the test be before you surrender? What is a test and who is testing you, someone seen, someone unseen? There is nobody testing you, save yourself. We are going to understand the term "master versus villager" and what is the difference between the two. The master has learned to be that which is called free space, to broaden the idea of acceptance from the senses to outside the senses. The master has learned to live in a world that is far vaster than the villager can conceive.

What is the job of the yellow brain, the neocortices? The yellow brain is that which is termed the virgin ground, the neocortex, the synaptic network yet to be formed in a new lifetime. It is a new start. There is some instinctual knowledge carried in the neurons through genetic makeup, but for the most part the yellow brain is an unmapped territory waiting to be explored, ready for a new life.

Contained within the yellow brain in all of you is the sum total of your personality. This simply means that the yellow brain houses everything that you know, what you have learned in this lifetime and your assessment of it, your judgment. Whatever you know is also in control of your emotional body, and your emotional body indeed is controlled in your physical body. What you think not only has lordship over your body but has lordship over your emotions and therefore lordship over your life.

If this neuronet in the yellow brain is the ground of your incarnation personality, this existence, then all of this neuronet is about what you believe in, what you know, and your assessments about what you believe in and what you know. For example, there are many things that you don't believe you can do. The reason that you don't believe you can do them is because you don't have any knowledge about them and yet you are the last one to admit it. You can't do them because you don't know how to do them.

You will never, ever venture outside of this box by the time you are past your puberty at thirty-two. The box is sort of an enigma. You can say, "Well, I went to this place and I went to that place and I had never been there before," but that is not venturing outside of the box because we already knew that those places existed. It was a matter of emotionally experiencing them before we got the experience of them, but we already knew they were there. We just didn't know how good they were or indeed how bad they were. We can also say, "Well, I know everything that I learned in school, such as it was, and I went on to higher education and only found out it was lower education, and I learned everything there. I know pretty much how to survive in a corporate world." That is still a box and I will tell you why, because you are never going to be any greater than what you know.

This is what is beautiful about the box and your personality. It is a safe haven. It is a place to which we can escape. In the box is contained all the neuronet of the sum total of our knowledge and our experiences. We carry with us certain arrogance, because as long as we have boundaries to our thinking we feel safe. It does not matter how corrupt it is inside the box. It doesn't matter how meanspirited you are or how unloving you are. It doesn't matter how great a victim you are. At least you are a victim and you can count on that. Well, that is living inside the box.

Believing in God is a safe thing because believing in God means that God is so big that it can never be explained, and that is safe. No one is ever asking you to say, well, what is God and what is God's relationship to you, as it were. It is safe not to know God because then you never have to explain it. We become victimized by the need for our own boundary, as it were, and indeed the need to be safe within that boundary. Villagers think the same way. They can predict any scene that they look upon, and they can understand any scene that they can look upon. No matter where you go in your life, any scene that you saw even up to this moment you could interpret and describe. Every scene that you have seen exists in your neuronet and you will never be able to see out there what doesn't first exist in your neuronet.

The Test of a True Master

The discipline of the master must be incorporated every day. In the case of what would make you radiantly healthy, for example, how many people have come up to you with a new vitamin supply that promises to give you radiant health? How many bizarre body disciplines are you going to do? How many times are you going to douche out your colon before you think that you have reached radiant health? If you were already radiantly healthy, it would already be in your neocortex, but it isn't. The test is, you keep going in and out trying to figure it out. You move all around the box. You think if you move, you have found the solution, only to move over there and see it from a different perspective. Then you find another piece of the puzzle, so you move to another part of your thinking. You think it to death because what happens is when everything fails that you have gone after, there is no rich aunt. There was a rich uncle, but he didn't leave it to you. Indeed the person that you thought liked you a lot and was going to give you some money, it turns out they don't have any to give. And no matter how many numbers you think you see in divine consciousness, they are all wrong at the gambling table.

The test is when you are pressed with your desire to the border of your neuronet, to the edge of your box. The test is when you stop utilizing people, places, things, times, and events because you already are them. You realize that that which is termed radiant health hasn't come by any medicinal claim, any dietary claim, or any exercise claim. When you have tried all of that, all the things you know, do you finally just become it or do you hit the edge of your box and give up in frustration?

The test of a true master is that they are radiant health. What does that mean? Every day before they get out of bed, they have already created the day regardless of the malady in their body. It does not matter how crippled they are, how many sores are open on their face, or if they have come to the end of their rope. They get up and create that they are filled with the love of God and that they radiate perfect health. When they create their day as being that, they walk ennobled, proud, without pain, and beautiful in their own countenance. They get up and look in that mirror and that is all they see. They may limp around the entire household and into the village, but in their mind they are radiant health and they don't give it up. They are not going to give up. Every night they live it and every day they live it. Everyone else gives up on them: "That poor miserable creature, why, he is as loony as a tick. He thinks he is well. Anyone in their right mind can see that he ain't well." That is true. Everyone in their right mind would never see that he was well. The only person seeing he is well is himself. It is his reality.

What happens one fine morning? One fine morning he has broken through the barrier of his own limitation, and he has walked the walk and lived it purely and simply. Here is the beautiful hand of God as consciousness and energy in full view, which brings about the miraculous healing. Ne'er you doubt. Why, you have seen it in this school. The entity goes to the mirror and doesn't see anything different. If the sore is gone and he doesn't walk with a limp, he does not see it any differently. It is the way it always was.

There are those that know that fabulous wealth can never be resolved upon the opinions of their own limited thinking, as it were. They realize this because they have exhausted every avenue to figure out how they were going to get it, and it all came to an ill end. That is enough to depress anyone. They would say, "Fabulous wealth, why don't I have it? Why don't I think I can have it? Maybe because I never understood that wealth is not about value. It is about the unlimited use of energy. If I can accept that I have an unlimited use of energy, that would be fabulous wealth, would it not?" So every day the entity embraces that they are fabulously wealthy. There is nothing in him or her that has to answer whether they deserve it any longer. That is no longer a question. Worth is not even a question, but the desire and the embracing of unlimited energy is worth going after. So be it.

What do they do? Every day they live as if it already is. Every day they enjoy a plethora of dreams that are rich in the opportunity of plenty and when the cup runs over, there is enough for everyone else. Then the dream gets sweeter and sweeter, and there is joy on the face of the dreamer. In that moment they are the richest person in the world, for the richest person in the world does not wear a face of joy such as this dreamer has this day. It does not matter every day if all that is left in the cupboard is stale bread, a bit of tea, and one last bit of jam. It does not matter — we are fabulously wealthy — because we are never going to ever pay tribute to lack again in any form. Now that is a master. That is what we are defining here this day because to each of you it is the opportunity of life and the will to contrive this life as you see fit. If all that you know is unfit to be lived, then you need more knowledge and you need more opportunity. There is the body, its humanity, its contrived personality, its heaviness, and its density, and then there is the sublime in us that is the God. It is the will. It is that which can be, when all body fails. It is that which is, when all logic runs dry. It is that which will persevere, when all faith has been lost. That is who I am after and that is who you are after.

In free space lives fabulous wealth, radiant energy, health, the ability to heal others, and love. "God, let us love and let us never stop. And the more that we love, the greater we give and the more God that we are. God, pray it never ends — never ends." That is a master that lives in free space. And what be free space? It is all the unlimitedness that I have taught you that exists on the other side of the thin wall of your thinking. How are you going to get there? How are you going to manifest it? You have to break through the box into free space. That means you must be it in spite of your programming, and when you are, your programming will change.

What does that take? It takes not giving up. Every day if we are left to that which is termed our natural biological thinking process, we will think only in terms of maintaining the box of safety: that we have enough to eat, we look good enough, indeed there is enough hot water, our automachines are clean and are bigger, faster, and badder, and where we labor in the marketplace is better than where the homeless live. If we leave ourselves to our image, we have a corruptible life. When we rise up and change that every day, we have a life that is sublime. Every day you cannot be sick, be weak, be the victim, and be poor. Every day you cannot suffer. Every day you must love, and every day you must be God. Is God in rags not a beautiful picture, an entity walking in a sublime mind, filled with the glory of free space, adorned in rags? That is only temporal.

When are you going to understand what it is that I am teaching you? When are you going to find that it is worth the time to be greater than your body, that you are greater than your body? When are you going to take control of your life, and I mean control of your life? When are you going to stop being the victim? You are only the victim because it serves you. In being a victim you can point to your poverty or your indebtedness and why you should worry. When are you going to give it up? When are you going to wake up and stop suffering and start living? You play with death and romance it because it is a companion for escape. I say to you it is easier to die than it is to live. No one who died was ever a hero. You are only a hero when you live through it. How much more ability do you need to be shown before you can accept what you can do? The maturation, as it were, of the humanoid to the master is a very fine line. When you want to, you will become it. Whose tests must you pass? Your own. What are they about? Just think about it. You have to be greater than what you think. That is all.

Free space is immediate because in free space there are no people, places, things, times, and events; therefore there is no judgment on it. Judgment is a delay. The moment you move into free space, you have it. The test is holding it in there in spite of all of your logic and figuring and bringing forth that divine self.

Then I ask you, what are you going to do for the rest of your life? If you cannot do this, then what will be the quality of your dreams the rest of your life? You are going to live by what you have inside of your brain, your neuronet, that little tiny bit of knowledge there, that very small experience with its habits and its victimization. This then is the agenda for the rest of your life, a boring life.

Being filled with the love of God, being filled with radiant health, having manifested fabulous wealth, what damage would that do to you if you did it every day? It doesn't take away from your day. Remember I told you the story about the entity who all of his life focused into his fire that he had all this great wealth and every day he lived his dream and shared it with those around him. Then when he died, everyone said, "Poor entity. He thought he was going to make the big one and he never did." But, you know, he was reborn and became the king of England at a very rich time in the aristocracy. It doesn't hurt; it enhances. You have nothing to lose except limitations by doing it.

Do you have what it takes to live beyond your own logic? Are you greater than your limitations, and when will you stop arguing for them? If you have thought about what I have said to you and asked yourself this, then we have changed the course of your life. When you understand that free space is a moment away, the moment that you are it without anything else — no matter what the mirror says, the body says, your pockets say — when you are that, in spite of it all, is when you get it.

Importance behind the Sacred Language of Symbology

In the biology of the brain, the job of the neocortices — the very fat and large brain that is mostly vacant — is to argue about thought and how it is presented because it is a house that is split apart. Thought comes up from the brainstem in electrical impulses through the nerve fibers that fire that which is termed the neurons of the neuronet in your brain. When they fire, pictures are made that have a buoyancy. A thought-form is a frozen formation of consciousness so that both juries can have commentary on it. This commentary is called judgment. As the pure form is presented, whether that is information coming from your body, information coming from your social-conscious atmosphere in which you are involved, or information coming from a future, all information presents itself in the neocortex totally pure. The body does not send conflicting information to the brain. The body does not have judgment. It responds, it gets its orders, it does what it is told, and it reports back to headquarters. All of the information coming from the body appears in the brain totally pure, virgin, and unhampered.

When the brain then formulates the information into thought-forms, you do not realize it because you have not observed your thoughts in slow motion. They are images that float, turn, and are beautiful. You will see that while they are turning, they start to fall apart. Their faces change, their angles change, the color changes, the proportion changes. As it turns and it changes, you would be mesmerized by the metamorphosis of the original thought to what it finally is allowed to become. If you could see this and how you do this, you would be utterly fascinated about the judge and jury that sit in the neocortex. Then as soon as it is disseminated, more thought-forms come up, and they are beautiful. They sit there, three-dimensional, rotating, changing, and then they disappear and more appear in their place. You can't see this because the thoughts are happening very rapidly in the brain and they are getting analyzed very rapidly.

This teaching is a presentation from a Lord, a God — me — presenting a pure code to you. The code has much more significance than the words. They are written a special way. They are sounded a special way. The reason they are sounded very peculiar is because the peculiarity of the sounds forms an utterly pure thought-form which the neocortex becomes baffled by because its formation is different from its ordinary information. What that means is that we create a hung jury. So be it.

You need to understand that the arcane teachings of antiquity, the great knowledge, was not written in symbols or stylized in a code to prevent outsiders from accessing it. The mystery of why it was stylized and presented in symbols and parables was for the entity for which it was meant. The code was given and the thought-forms appeared in the recipient's brain, to the astonishment of the jury. The jury cannot analyze the code, and when it cannot analyze the code then the original intent stays pure. It is tricking ourselves into greatness, but whatever works, works.

Purity comes into the brain as pure water but because it is filtered through a dirty cloth of common thought, what comes through the dirty cloth is dirty water. That is the way consciousness is affected once we get through with it. It comes out as altered, judged, changed, and convoluted. It in turn convolutes one's life to the point that we accept this convolution as utterly normal because we have never understood how our body and our brain have been culturally designed to work to present a reality that is cohesive for everyone. It is designed that way.

Common thought is the most powerful thought that you have. I want you to listen very carefully to how simple this message is. Those thought-forms you just start thinking in a train of thought that rolls out of you are common thoughts that have already been altered, discerned, judged, and changed. The reason they come out of you pell-mell is because they are the finished product of your brain and they issue forth randomly. Whatever is given permission to be discharged into the frontal lobe is reality. How do you hold this ridiculous reality in place? By your ridiculous thinking, and the ridiculous thinking has the power of common thought. It just recycles itself and goes out. It is allowed to go out because it is already judged. It is already altered. It has been given permission. It is what you think normal thinking is all about, but that is powerful thinking. This is your mystical power of what you would never see but is there with you every day. Think about that for a moment, because how else do we explain or justify your ability to create reality?

You are already red in the rainbow. When I endeavor to talk about red, you have no idea what I am talking about because you are already it. You are analogically the color. It is the only color you will never see. Consequently, when I talk about your power, it is the only power you will never see because you are already it in common thinking. Common thoughts are reaffirming the reality of monkey-mind, living in the box, settling for the neuronet that is holding your life together. By removing people, places, things, times, and events from a pure thought of focus, you are allowing the pure thought to turn and move in its purity of form inside the brain, holding back the judgment, the alteration, the degradation, and the limitation of the thought-form that normally would change and destroy its original meaning so that it could fit within the box and then be sent out. When we hold such glorious thoughts without assessing them or tying them into a person, a place, a thing, a time, or an event, we cannot judge because these are the bases of our judgment and indeed our prejudice. We are holding the jury mute. This pristine thought-form dances then like a beautiful flame in the center of your brain, for the code allows it to stand. If it is held there in its purity for an extended period of time, it will be conceived as common thought and it will go out from you, which will be as insignificant as the insignificant thoughts that you have every day of your life.

The knowledge hereto that you have gained and the concept that you focus upon have been very significant, highly relevant, and very important. It is what you really want, and you are so afraid you are not going to get it. You have a lot of reason to be afraid because you are usually the one that tears it down and destroys it. You don't know that you are doing that because you are red in the rainbow. You are looking for some tyrant out there to blame for the loss of your idealism or the loss of your dream when in reality you are the tyrant. It is what you are doing to it.

We take this beautiful, important dream, "I want to be a master. I want it so desperately. This is what I want above everything else and, God help me, I mess it up at every turn. Why? What is my block?" You are your block because you have made this desire so important it cannot stand up against the test of your monkey-mind. You will tear it down until it fits within the mold of your acceptance because you cannot accept being a master. That is the way it works. You have made these dreams so important that you try so hard to hold the focus, you try so hard to be righteous, and you try so hard to keep that focus that you are so intense and your body is in stress. What happens then is the longer and the more you try, the greater the breakdown of the dream because it is too important for it to become common thought.

The really important things in your life will very rarely ever be manifested because they are so important they are not even you. They lie outside of the realm of your common process, and until they can be common to you, they will never occur. That is why it is important to be unlimited and that being unlimited is the nature of your being. If you focus upon doubt and remove people, places, things, times, and events from doubt, it can't stay because the only reason you have doubt is because it is attached to one of these things. If you remove those things, doubt does not exist. If you focus upon the lack of your self-worth and focus on lack without attaching it to a person, a place, a thing, a time, an event, it disappears because lack cannot exist unless it is attached to one of these. It is a judgment in the brain. It is the same way with illness. If you focus upon an illness without placing it in any of the categories, it cannot live in that environment.

Secret Teachings of the Ancient Schools of Wisdom

I know how to talk to your mind. I know it very well. I understand how the mechanics of your thinking work. I see so clearly what you have done to your life by arguing for your limitations and insisting upon your rational mind. I have watched you. You are your greatest testament to the power that you have within you. I am taking you on an adventure to show you that masters do not make a big deal out of the awesomeness of their being because to them it is common thought. What else could it be? That is the reply that you will get, but to get you to be this awesome in the very limited way that you have lived before is going to be an arduous task.

When you create your day in the morning, form the thought of how you want the day, and command your holy Holy Spirit that it is so, the whole day must obey common thought and it rolls out in front of you. If that commandment and holding that pure thought-form is without emotion, then it is commonly accepted. But it is not going to happen because you did it five days and somehow that is going to carry you on for the rest of the year. It has to be done every day. When you understand the code, you will engage the discipline every single day, and to your sheer delight you will find yourself commonly thinking in terms of a master. It will not be spectacular. It will not be extraordinary. It will be a God, and therein lies the difference. You won't have to try. You will just be it. This then catapults the serious student into a whole new level of understanding.

In the ancient schools this aspect of the learning was never taught. There was no way to teach the student about common thought because it wasn't a term, and so much allegory was presented in order to describe it. There really wasn't a term for social consciousness either. What you have learned about removing people, places, things, times, and events is a new teaching, as well as the understanding of the uncorrupted thought and the term "common thought." No one understood common thought before. Many would be students of the Great Work all of their lives, but few of them ever became adepts at it because the missing ingredient was this complexity which kept escaping them. They had the knowledge and they could engage the discipline, but there was something missing. There was something that they were not seeing. What they were not seeing was what they were being analogically.

When you think that the brain is the sitting judge and jury and these pure thoughts come up and become corroded, we begin to understand how gas pain in the chest — because the great intestine is right behind the cardiovascular system — how that information coming to the brain could be judged as a heart problem. If it is judged that, then it will become that. It is the way reality works. We begin to understand how the great among you will accept commonly that which is termed the opportunity of fabulous wealth, remarkable mind, living eternally, not having to die, the concept of never aging again, the concept of utter and total power, control over the elements as your endowment without any argument and without any hesitation. It will become the basis by which you think. Others, it will always escape you.

If I can make God to you as common as fixing the brakes on your automachine and get you to think that way, you will have it all: immortality, fabulous wealth, being filled with the power of the Holy Spirit, seeing and knowing all. Then you will have made the breakthrough of all time that only a few have ever broken through. It is a matter of getting up every day with breath like jasmine blooming in the morning and being excited about life, excited about the prospects of the day, excited about being alive. Instead of waking up with wretched, poisonous breath, you wake up smelling like a flower because suddenly you are alive and you are not dying. The day is precious, is beautiful, and you cannot wait to get up, engage it, and create it in common thought. It will be your passion. And as your day rolls through, it is just what it is. Who is the source of that? You. And every day gets better and better and better, and the adventures at night become sweeter and sweeter. Now you will know why we live forever. There are those of you who think about taking your life. You are already dead, and you have already been dead. Who could think about removing their life when they have never lived? This is life. You have thought it into very mundane boxes. I am teaching you to see that there is no end to it.

How many of you have had something happen to you and instead of reacting to it emotionally with a commonality of hysteria, suddenly you were in the midst of a great calm and simply knew what to do? That is free-space common thought. That is the way you are supposed to be. When we begin to analyze the miraculous with a lesser mind, we always carve the miraculous down to fit the way that we think, commonly and limitedly, and by the time you do that it has lost its mystique, its beauty, its adventure, and its change along with its challenge. We could say that is indeed a tragedy in human terms. I want you to understand that everything I am teaching you should not be viewed in a mode of hysteria as being so far out that it is unattainable. One day when you get to speak to a real master you will ask them questions with bated breath and you will expect them to respond in some sort of fanatical, cosmic way. It will be difficult to hold a conversation with them because they speak about what you consider miraculous in very normal, accepted terms. "What else could it be?" they would say to you. "How else is there to live? If I have created the illness, who better to heal it than I?" That is how they talk. You can't drag any victimization out of them. It will be a shock to you because you will understand that the way they are talking is really equal to the way that you talk every day except the difference is lifetimes. So be it.

A Master's Road Map — The List

I want you to go over these affirmations:

I am filled with the radiant power of the Holy Spirit.
I am thirty years younger (or five years older).
I am perfect health.
I am never aging another day.
I manifest in the palm of my hand instantly
  whatsoever I want.
I am fabulous wealth.
I know the thoughts of others.
I manifest at will all that I need.
I heal others and myself.
I am thirty pounds lighter (or thirty pounds heavier).

If you are acutely interested in these forming in your mind, I want you to read them out loud very slowly and unemotionally. You are to say all of these with passion but without emotion just as mundanely as the things that you think, but do it with direction. They are commanding the brain to move into action, and it would appear to the subconscious back here that the jury upstairs has reached a decision and now they are giving orders. When you talk to the subconscious mind it seems like you are talking to a child, and you are, because the mind of God is like a child. When you talk to it, it does not argue back at you. It holds all the secrets, all the knowledge of who you have been, everything that you have done, and has the agenda already worked out in correlation with the soul. It knows everything. Yet when you talk to it you get the feeling that you are talking to the most awesome being, but it is in the body of a child because it is so sweet. It will answer you. It will not argue with you. It will engage readily what you ask it, and it will make it manifest. It is the power that created universes.

It never voices its opinion, like most children never voice their opinion. The subconscious mind is God as a child, and here we have the ridiculous mature mind that has to squabble on petty issues before it will even converse with a child and rarely ever does. In this code, we are conversing with the subconscious mind, the powerful child. In the case of body weight, when you say "I command you," it will say "So be it" and will regulate your body straightaway to lose your body weight. Your body metabolism and your body heat will increase in one night. The fidgety energy that you will wake up with the next day is a result of that God going to work. You will also find that you will want to eat the food that this God has determined this body needs. If you go and counter your own claim to it, it will allow you to do that but it will keep the orders up as long as you tell it to do so. The day that you wake up and don't tell it to do so, it will stop. It is there to serve you, but it knows so much more than you do and its power is without measure.

When the God within you is told to gain weight, it will do that. It will slow the body's metabolic rate down. It will take the food and it will not burn it rapidly, for a nervous metabolism is what does that. The fuel that is taken into the body will not be burned up in anxiety any longer. It will be stored. It will do exactly as you ask it to do because it is the God of this body. It will do it because it knows that you have reached a decision. Common thought is the decision you have reached every day that causes this child to act upon what you think. Common thought is its law.

We are addressing the God within. That is why this is spoken the way it is and is paying apt, rapt attention to it. It goes to work immediately. There is no delay when we invoke it. I want this part to be important to you because I want you to invoke the power within you so that you know what you are sitting upon in your brain. I also want you to understand that the child in you, the great God within you, also accesses free space. Here is the dilemma. When we purport confusion and we take the wonderful and break it down into analytical jargon, we are so busy analyzing and conjecturing potentials that we never give it to the God within to do anything, so it lies there in free space unused. We want to access what is in free space. We get the unused potentials in free space only when we reach for them without emotionally judging or altering them to fit our own agenda, our own criteria of belief. When we simply accept it, then this is put into immediate action. The reason why the beautiful lies outside instead of inside your brain is because you have never taken it in. The beautiful lies uncorrupted out there.

Every possible miracle you could ever think about that you could have is a moment away, and the only way you get it is when you take it without alteration. When we talk to the God within, it listens to us and accepts our opinion and our direction. It thinks we have reached a conclusion.

It doesn't know that what is given to it has not already gone through the process. It just does it. What I want you to experience is how close your God is and how rapidly transformation happens when we take this thought-form, this List that I have created for you, hold it absolutely pure, and use it to command the God within you to change and to alter whatever is on your List.[1]

Health is always perfect to the God within you because the state of being who you are is exactly what you have asked to be, so it considers it perfect. It is only giving you the body from the orders that you hand down in every thought that you have. You have to inform it differently. According to the God within, you have a biological clock ticking. It is genetically predisposed for a life span, taking into consideration the hostile environment in which you exist. This God within already knows the time of your death and is already prepared for it. By the time that you have reached twenty-one years of age, the death hormone is already being secreted in your body from that which is termed the great seventh seal. It is already moving in your body. The death hormone turns off the ability of the cells to live forever and starts the eroding process of degeneration. It is exactly in line with your culture, it is exactly in line with what you think, and it is exactly in line with a bunch of people who are nothing more than a bag of chemicals that worship themselves. In the List we have addressed health, body weight, nutrition, and being unlimited. We have said to the God within us that we want to engage free space. Free space means unlimited mind. In the presence of that which is termed the Holy Spirit, you are commanding your body to have radiant energy. Why

_____

1 "I am perfect health; I am fabulous wealth; I know the thoughts of others," et cetera. The List is a discipline taught by Ramtha where students learn to focus on a list of items they choose and desire to become and experience in their lives. See also Changing the Timeline of Our Destiny, Fireside Series, Vol. 1, No. 2 (Yelm: JZK Publishing, 2001). The Neighborhood Walk[SM] taught by JZ Knight and Ramtha is an evolved version of this discipline.

wouldn't the God within you listen to that? You are commanding it. The child will do exactly what you say. It will not argue with you. It will command you to have radiant energy. The day that you wake up and are too tired to command your God to have radiant energy is the day you won't have it. You would say, "I am just too tired, too tired to get up and command radiant energy. I don't think I can handle radiant energy today." No problem, you won't get it. Go back to sleep. That is how it works.

The List I gave you is a timeline. It is a road map that every day affirms you on the timeline and sets as manifestation each one of these events to be fulfilled in the course of your progression. This is the List of destiny. When it is done every single day it overrides and curbs the genetic list of destiny, which you genetically carry in every cell in your body and to which your hormones respond. It also overrides any thinking and attitudes you had that kept you on a timeline before you learned the List. This List done every day keeps you on a journey and keeps you from wavering off of it.

Listen to me, my beautiful people. You are not the first who ever had the sacred map. This is the sacred map, which seems very simple, very cosmopolitan, very normal, but it is a sacred List. It is what every great adept has used to manifest not only an eternal life but the desires they wished to manifest in evolution. Every adept understands that all the potentials of their life are existing every moment and in order to reach the epic destiny they desire, they must incorporate a map. Invoking the map every day puts them on a timeline and allows them to experience these things. They only put on the List what they desire to experience. This here is very much a neophyte List. A master has already done all of these things. You can only imagine what their map looks like, but they have already done all of this. They have already reached the age that they wish to hold. They have already lived longer than two hundred and fifty years. They are full-bore aware psychics. They can transcend time and matter, bilocate anywhere they want to be, go forward and backwards in time, and they started with this List. Understand the List in terms of common thought, your thinking every day. Those thoughts, those words that roll out of you have already been carved down by the judge and jury sitting up here in the brain. Masters accept that this List is common thought. This is the law. It comes out of you and it reaffirms your destiny.

Every day that you get up and you feel bad, you are going to be bad. Every day you get up and say, "I don't have any energy," you are not going to have any energy. Every moment during the day if you judge someone else, you will be judged. If you doubt yourself for a moment during the day, you will have every experience show you why you should. If during the day you have fantasies of dying, then you are going to have a meeting with death. If every day you think rotten thoughts about someone else, those thoughts are on their way back to you because you are on the timeline to meet them. Now that is the way it works. If you get hung up in an attitude or a habit and that is all you seek, if you are in your first three seals and that is the only thing that you think about, you are on a timeline to meet all the destiny involved with that.

No one puts you in the Prancing Pony Inn. You end up there by self-choice. No one puts you in a bed of disease. You end up there by choice in the matrix of your common-thought thinking. Understanding the power of incorporating the List daily, very soon you start to think like the List. You will see the God in everyone. You will find the beauty in all people. You will love and be the giver of love without asking for it in return. You will find that every day you will start to commonly think as this List, and when you do, now you are on its timeline and it is manifesting every single day.

It is easy. You can choose to get up in the morning and trust your own thinking process to give you a good day and trust your own reactions through the day to sort of set the mood for the evening and tomorrow morning. You can trust your own thinking to see if you can ride it out for the next five years. You can see if your thinking is good enough to keep you from harm's way in the next five years. You can trust that thinking or you can do this List. Then very soon, like all great masters, you start to think like the List, and when you do, what else can it do but manifest your life accordingly.

Most people are brought up to believe that imagination is some sort of side effect of human emotion and that it shouldn't be taken for real. Well, that is an idiotic teaching. The gift of imaging is exactly how reality is created, not only in your personal life but with that which is termed society and cultures as a whole. Every culture existing within the world that you can name, both present and past, all were created through a network of philosophical theories and dreams. They didn't just spring about; they were created intentionally. In your modernized world, there is a threat to do away with the mind of man and woman in the context of the dreaming mind, the dreaming consciousness, because it is not seen as being technically wise. I say to you that without the dreaming consciousness of man and woman, technology as it is so celebrated now would not have been invented. It is like the child trying to destroy the mother.

There are many people who have dreams and desires but they don't have the passion to get them. Passion is the desire to hold them ever in the forefront of your consciousness, to be able to move through the labyrinth of mundane days of suffering and boredom and not give up your dreams. That is passion. Everyone dreams, but very few have the passion to see them through.

The Initiate's Labyrinth and the Beach of Tranquillity

The beautiful shore of the beach of tranquillity was the site of the greatest labyrinth that was ever built. It has existed in a holy and secret place throughout the ages. The labyrinth was underground and ran through the chambers of an entire mountain range. The labyrinth was the greatest test ever devised for initiates. Its path was underground rivers and water, and it was blacker than night. Those who survived had to know and hold their own without panic, without emotion, claustrophobia, fear of darkness, fear of water, fear of the unknown, fear of falling, and fear of dying. Those who were fearless and had already plotted the end of the test were the few initiates who survived this great test.

After moving through the bowels of an entire mountain range through the pathways of water, sometimes rapid and harsh with only an inch or two for breath between the top of the water and the top of the cave, they were washed up exhausted. They had to know when to come up for air, when not to come up, and with no preparation at all to make a long fall into a dark cavern falling with water. Those who survived flowed out of the underground stream onto this beautiful sand. They were washed right onto the shore of a tranquil lake, a large body of water fed by the stream. They would lie there still transfixed into their trance, still existing in their midbrain, still holding the dream, and yet they had come through the greatest test upon which they had ever been tested. There their exhausted bodies lay completely surrendered to the white sand and the gentle surf lapping back and forth upon their feet. It was sweet. It was like the kiss of nature that caressed their feet, their legs, their knees, and their hips. It would rush all the way over to their face and mingle with their tears. They wept and had the most profound faith in themselves because they had survived the test. Then nature caressed and loved them.

This was a magical area. There was always a mist, a great cloud that liked to sleep upon the mountain, and then when it got particularly lazy it would fall down near the shoreline as a lazy cloud. I daresay it is the same one that was there twenty thousand years ago. It hasn't gone anywhere. It likes where it is. This beautiful cloud lay upon the distant horizon of this body of water. The water would reflect the cloud, the cloud would reflect the water, and they became the same. It would look as if this body of water had no break and it was the vault of heaven itself. As the initiates lay there not moving, with sand that was beginning to collect on their eyelashes and salt that was drying on their faces, they saw this beautiful mist roll in with the waves as they came up and back and then receded, as though a sweet whisper. Then this beautiful fog would come over them and they would inhale the cloud itself and then exhale it. It was rejuvenation and it was a time of quiet in which the initiates were allowed to lie there for as long as they chose.

This beach of water still exists even in what you call this modern century and has been protected by that long lazy cloud that has never left. The great labyrinth is still alive and well, and only a few through an entire century are ever brought there and have ever gone through it. This is the story of great ones, and this is where they ended up.

GROWING THE SEEDS OF
ALTERNATIVE TIMELINES OF POTENTIAL

My greatest teacher in my lifetime was nature. Having seven years of doing nothing but sitting and observing the coming and going of night and day and realizing all the life that belonged to those hours, I became a very astute student of nature. I understood indeed that nature was the very Unknown God of my people and that I had finally found it. The Unknown God wasn't a being. It was all life in general. The natural order of this world, even back 35,000 years ago, is the same nature that is at work today as the seasons change and the cool air fights for dominance over the hot air. From winter's sleep come the dreams of winter bursting forth into the warm air of spring. All the flowers that you see, all the buds and the green growth that you see, all belonged to the dream of that plant in the time of winter, and all that you see around you came from a seed.

If we become astute observers of nature, we will understand indeed the greatest cosmology we could ever want to know about the righteousness of things and how they grow. We would understand then our own processes, because everything abides by these natural laws that are invoked upon this plane. Whether it is a mustard seed or the sperm and egg coming together to make a human being, the seed has laws with which it must abide in order for life to flourish.

The seed looks nothing like its potential, what it will eventually become. Who could say what this seed will become if we were to remote-view the mustard seed or the seed of celery that are barely visible? You would really have to know the craft in order to get it correct, because the monkey-mind would look at it and not have a clue. As far as it is concerned, a mustard seed would be very similar to grains of sand on a beach. Then the monkey-mind would immediately think that this came from some groundwork or beachwork, which shows you how much it knows. The seed holds the promise of something much more extraordinary, the chain of life's renewal.

If you have ever observed seeds, they don't do too well if they are just out lying around on counters, on floorboards, on your dressers and bureaus in bags. They can be sitting there for years and still look like the same old seed. In my way of thinking, that is sort of like our thoughts and our dreams that could lie around for years. We can have the most illustrious thought in the world, but if it is not germinated it is not going to go anywhere. When we put the seed and cover it in its natural soil — and you could even take a little seed, a mustard seed, put it on the surface and then cover it with a rock — it will immediately turn on. What is the key ingredient to the seed? Darkness. Isn't that wonderful? The most condemned opposite of light turns out to be the giver of light.

If you take any seed, put it under a rock or a rotten log, hide it under an old smelly tennis flopper, and go out and check within a night of eight hours or check the next day, you will see that the seed is marginally fatter. If you check it another night or the next morn, you will see it is even fatter than it was the night before. If you check it in three days, you will see it has little legs coming out of it. The rest is history.

The metamorphosis of a seed holds within it a specific dream — a specific dream — and that dream holds within it its continuity. In other words, inside the seed lies not only the dream of its flowering but the dream of its immortality. Inside the seed is not only the flower but generations of flowers to come, in one seed. What must we do? We must obey the law of nature by putting it in a dark place, in dark earth. The earth has microorganisms of nutrients that neutralize the first sprout, the very first microscopic sprout. This is important because the first sprout needs the first minute molecules to turn on the internal engine that brings the sprout further into being. While it lies in darkness, it creates a neuronet of roots. The neuronet of roots becomes its foundation. As soon as the neuronet of the root line is laid and the inner manufacturing plant is set up and all the proper entities hired, then it breaks the surface because the next key ingredient is gentle heat. Gentle heat can come from the solar rays penetrating the womb around the Earth, magnifying them, and creating the friction of heat, or gentle heat can be a magnetic heat from the magnetic fields of the Earth itself. Magnetic friction gives heat. When the root line is ready, then it only takes gentle heat which can be from the sun and its rays magnified through the screen around the Earth or through that which is termed the Earth's magnetic field. It breaks the surface, and all it needs after that is the heat and water. That is all it needs. From this pitiful little seed will come about a magnificent plant that is so huge, and then it will produce. Have you ever wondered where did it get all of the stuff to become so big? I did.

My night bird stayed in a flowering bush, which was beautiful, but when it didn't flower, it was a scrub of a bush. It was rather an ugly, tangled, web-looking thing sitting there with some thorns. The night bird liked that because it protected its nest from predators, even me. But that ugly, web-looking scrub of a bush with those thorns would produce the most exquisite crimson flower, and it smelled beautiful, like if you mingle the subtle scents of hibiscus and jasmine. I had nothing else better to do but watch this ugly bush give me a beautiful show. I got to see how this gray, barky thing made a crimson flower that had perfume. Isn't that wonderment? I had a long time to think about that because every season it was taking over my space. I loved it too much. It grew in and around me. It was a great teacher to me, and I thought about the metamorphosis of the hormonal body in the nature of things. The flower blooms and in its blooming it has also created and regenerated itself in the form of seed and pollen so the seed can be carried and germinated to fall into someone else's hand and have them wonder the same thing, for that seed has perpetuated immortality. We can use then the analogy that winter is the time that the seed sleeps and rests. When it is cold, it doesn't grow. When it is in a cold ground, it dreams. It absolutely does. A mustard seed has consciousness and it dreams, and when all conditions are correct, then the dream comes into fruition.

"I am filled with vital energy" is a seed. We as human beings in the here-and-now know all of those words or can translate them into the various languages. They have been hanging around a long time. When we put them together into a cohesive present statement, "Vital energy I am," they become very powerful potentials. How do we propagate vital energy into an ugly gray brambling bush that you are and make a crimson flower blossom? We have to take the seed and give it to the brain. The only way that this seed will get propagated into the human brain is when the human brain is covered in darkness. The brain is actually in light when it is being fed the neurotransmitter serotonin, the daytime neurotransmitter, and it shuts everything off when it is fed melatonin, the nighttime transmitter. As the earth becomes the activator for the seed to start growing and producing its neuronet root-work, melatonin provides the fertile environment of darkness so that this saying can become cohesive and its groundwork is formed. It must have a neuronet and must be complete. Right now you could say, "But I have all those words in my brain, so I have a neurological hookup to 'I' and 'am' and 'fertile' and 'vital' and all of that." That is true; otherwise we could not know these words or what they represent. When we unify those neuronets together, we create a web-work, an actual root system. This is how we emulate nature.

By looking at you, "I am vital energy" so far isn't a root-work in your body because if it were, you would have vital energy right now because that would be the neurological net that is firing in that brain. If you had the root system of this seed in place, you wouldn't be tired because every time I say "vital energy" you would be shining, and you are not. We have to establish the seed in darkness to multiply and bring about the root system.

Melatonin and serotonin are produced mainly in the brain by the sixth seal, the pineal gland. The pineal gland is hooked right up to the eye. In other words, the same cells that occupy the pineal gland also occupy the eye. Many people have construed that the third eye is the pineal gland looking through the eye. There is truth to that. It is measuring light and darkness, and the moment the eyes are covered and see no light, the pineal gland will transmute serotonin into melatonin. Melatonin slows you down and puts you in stillness. It is the precursor to pinoline, which is deep sleep. When it slows you down, it will allow you to move into Twilight®, a vivid dreaming state. In order to set the root system of any seed in the brain, we must have darkness. The darkness emulates the seed going into the earth. When you say "I am filled with vital energy" and every word is present and focused, the image attached to it is the flowering of the seed.

The most important thing is being righteous about doing the List properly early in the morning and late at night. "It is what I want to manifest in my life. It is the map of my enlightenment and longevity." If you treat it with that sort of preciousness and do it correctly, you will form the root system. It is the new timeline. In other words, the body will turn into vital energy because the neuronet is there and the flower is blooming. If you don't do it, then the seed lies around for a hundred years. It is never planted in fertile soil and it is never given gentle heat in order for it to break the surface. So you don't deserve any of this because you haven't set the root system. You have not, in essence, followed the law of nature itself. You are not wiser than nature. How do I know that? Because for many of you, those trees outside this door were around before you were born and for the youngest of you will still be growing in their youth when you meet your death. Now who is the wisest, you or that tree? It is the tree, because the tree only knows how to live, and if we look at it, it will teach us many wonderful things.

Are you sick? Are you crippled? Are you lame? Are you stupid? Are you slow? Are you uncouth? No matter what you think you are, it can all be changed by planting the right seeds in the brain and flowering them consciously and chemically in the body. Are you tired of being sick? Then change it. Are you tired of being slow? Change it. Are you tired of growing old? Change it. Plant the seed and let it flower, and do it every day.

If you have a little difficulty doing this, think about my bush, that thorny, gray, weblike mass that a beautiful bird for generations lived in and sang to me all night long and how something so scruffy could produce such a beautiful flower. Think about this. If we are going to change our bodies in any way, the change in the body must be a chemical change. In other words, the body is a bag of chemicals. The plant, that bush, was a bag of chemicals, the same as me. The only difference between us was the program in the seed. That was the only difference. That plant and I are very close because we share the same frequency and we share nearly the same chemical base. What made me different was my genetic tree, my DNA. My DNA was set up differently than the plant's DNA, but we both share DNA. I was set up differently through different positive and negative poles producing molecular chemicals as a chemical mass that is different from the plant's, but we share the same DNA. Interesting, isn't it?

This is what I want you to understand. What brought

about that crimson flower out of that woody, tangled mess was that the flower emerged from the chemical state of that woody mess, the chemicals for red and velvet texture with a white mouth, yellow stamen, and a perfume that was intoxicating. I tell you, when that plant bloomed at night and that bird sang, I was in bliss. I was assailed by the most beautiful music I had ever heard, besides a flute player in battle, and the most intoxicating smell that women in all their cleverness could never have emulated.

So how did it produce that flower? I asked myself these questions. It came to me in an enlightenment that we share the same chemicals. The flower is made up of the same chemical process that is in the woody texture of the bush itself. What transmuted those chemicals to produce this flower in an array of color, texture, design, and chemical perfume was a program in the seed. I understood that the consciousness in the seed is the same consciousness I share and that it had decided to bloom. This was its design and its destiny. When it decided to bloom as a program in the seed, that decision coming from a conscious being upon its nervous system sent the signals to dissolve the former and rearrange growth. Dissolving the former meant that it dissolved from its own body those chemical makeups that would re-form to form the flower, its texture, its color, and its perfume. It was consciousness that did it. Think about this. The flower came from the bark and the bark came from a seed, each built upon through consciousness.

What I want to tell you, my beloved people, is that you are not beyond redemption in the body, meaning you are not helpless when it comes to death and the biological clock. You are also not helpless when it comes to the destructive power of your emotional instinct upon your parents' genetic acceptance. Stress will bring about cancer in the body. It was programmed that way. You are not helpless, and with knowledge you can understand how to change that. We have some outrageous seeds upon this List.[2] I am telling you that you can even plant the seed to turn back time in your body and bring it back to perpetual youth. Perpetuity of your mortal state, which means you can live for two hundred and fifty years, is an outrageous statement. I tell you there are masters that have been alive for 35,000 years and have never died. That miracle is the same miracle as a crimson flower coming from the bark of a scrubby bush. It is the same miracle.

All of these things you can become. When the root system is set properly within the brain, the neuronet clicks in. Common thought, when you least expect it, will issue forth one of these sayings in your mind, and you start laughing for joy because when it becomes common thought for you, it is the seed that has been planted. An incorruptible body will be formed out of the same chemicals from the corruptible body, out of the same DNA, out of the same electrical system. It is never too late. I don't care if you are ninety-nine years old, you have the power to turn back your body to the time you were ten years old. All we have to do is plant the seed and be diligent that it stays in darkness and that it is given gentle heat to start to bloom. The gentle heat comes in our laughter.

When we suddenly produce this saying out of common thought, and we catch the common thought, it is the joy of our being that is the accepted love of what we have planted in winter and is about to bloom in spring. There is no one that cannot be regenerated to any age they so desire, and there is no one who has lost their hair that by genetic code cannot grow it back. You all can. There is no one whose eyes have been damaged that cannot regenerate new eyes and new vision, new hearing, new hearts, new organs, and new limbs because they are chemicals. You walk around

---

2 See a variety of examples in the appendix of *Changing the Timeline of Our Destiny*, Fireside Series, Vol. 1, No. 2 (Yelm: JZK Publishing, 2001).

looking the baggy way that you do because you are a product of your thinking. Look at you. Your body tells everything about who you are and the way that you think. It doesn't take a mystic to know. It is obvious.

I love a spirited man and I love a righteous woman. A spirited man is one whose will is so strong that it is greater than ten thousand broadswords, and no matter the heat of the battle he will never give in and you will never get him. If you try to take his life, you will never get him. He will never recant. That is a willful, spirited man I love and is the substance of greatness. A righteous woman is a woman who takes the right use of knowledge and applies it with vigor every day. No matter how bare the cupboard, the righteous woman knows that it is filled. That is a righteous woman, and that is why they take care of the home, the hearth, and the children so well because given their care, there is nothing that will put asunder those in their charge. That is a righteous woman. Righteousness and being spirited are the innate qualities of both genders, but it takes a truly remarkable being in this day in your time to have either because your technology has made you fat and lazy. The overabundance of food has made you careless about the hearth and those in your care. A spirited man is hard to find because he is locked into his lower seals and very rarely has the spirit of determination about him. What it takes to turn the seed into the flower is the spiritedness of the one who will hold this and cultivate the garden, plant the seeds, till its earth, keep its weeds out daily so the garden will bear fruit. It does not matter what anyone else is doing. It does not matter if the entire earth is barren, they will have the garden. This means that the one who is dedicated to the flowers of God sees itself as the whole garden and will tend it daily and make certain it grows. The righteous woman who is the picker of the flower will make certain that these seeds are planted and bear fruit for the responsibility and love that is engendered within them.

All we need is to put this into action and then we have ninety-year-old people returning to their youth, sick people regenerating their organs, blind people who are seeing, deaf people who are hearing, and closed-dimensional people who are now open, and all because they tended the garden. I love it, because how much more outrageous was the desire of becoming the wind? When I observed the flowering bush and I saw from its side this flower came with its perfume, don't you think I realized at the end of seven years I could do anything because all I had to do was change it in my mind and my body would follow in hot pursuit? How do you think you become the wind? The same process, that is how.

The Greatest Deterrent, a Guilty Conscience

It is very difficult to manifest in the kingdom of heaven with a guilty conscience or a heavy conscience. A heavy conscience usually means that when your conscience is bothering you, you have done something unpardonable to someone else: You have undermined them, betrayed them, talked falsely about them, used them, or you have abused them. Abuse does not come at the tip of a sword, a cat-o'-nine-tails, a short-sword, battle-ax, saber, cannon, or nuclear warhead. Abuse can be a very subtle weapon in hurting someone else. You cannot do this work in a heavy conscience. When your conscience is bothering you, it will be the greatest deterrent for the Great Work because it means that your soul is alarmed at your behavior and your soul knows that you have gone off track. This pain or aching in the soul, in your chest where it belongs, sends messages up through the lower cerebellum, the subconscious. They start coming out in your dreams because that is when the subconscious has an opportunity to heal the body but also heals the soul. It gives you dreams and portents that are endeavoring to reflect to you the error of your ways. People have trouble sleeping because they are troubled by their dreams. During the day most people suppress a conscience that bothers them, cover it up, and use the term self-lack, self-worth. That is how it is transformed in the neocortex, that you don't feel worthy enough to do the work. The feeling of self-worthiness and the lack thereof is really an intellectual arrangement of the soul's warning, an alarm system that you have betrayed, undermined, or otherwise been harmful to someone else. You justify that indirectly in the conscious mind — never directly — and the warning signs are indirectly the lack of self-confidence and self-worth, which then deter the focus. The focus never really goes to an analogical state because there is a sense in you that you are not worthy of it.

I want to tell you something: God is love. God is a giver, not a taker. When we take from the dignity and the esteem of others, we are not godlike. When we undermine the stability, the fruitfulness, the beauty, the kindness, the overall wholeness of another individual, we are not acting as God; we are acting as wretched creatures. The wretchedness of our being then is what prevents us from manifesting the kingdom of heaven. This is where we find the key to long-term depression. The entity somewhere along the way has been injurious to another entity, has suppressed it, and has formed itself as the lack of self-esteem in human consciousness. That is why they never feel they ever deserve joy or happiness because they are denying themselves a simple confession of what they dare not say that they have done for the sake of pride. Pride is such a very powerful creature that it can keep you from the kingdom of heaven. It can keep you from manifesting God's most wonderful abundance. It can keep you from having a long and fruitful life and it will make you old before your time.

The greatest we can do is to understand that when we act as God, we act as givers. We give. Giving doesn't mean that you are a fool. Giving means giving everyone room to be who they are, giving everyone understanding, giving everyone hope, because that is what you need. When you give to people in this sort of measure that is godlike, then you are giving to them exactly what the soul is asking for yourself. Then we are righteous beings. We are righteous, the right use of human consciousness. When we go to sleep we are not troubled by our dreams. We are not fearful of what the night brings or the day brings. We sleep in sweet repose knowing that we languor in the bosom of God and that we have harmed no creature, nor have we undermined any human or made the path for someone more arduous or more difficult. Whatever we focus upon we can say that we are clear, and we can move into an analogical focus straightaway because we are worthy to do so. And who said we are worthy? We ourselves, the greatest judge and jury there are, one you can never escape.

What indiscretion has anyone done that is so great as to keep you from enjoying the fruits of your Father's kingdom? What have they done that is so great that it would cause you to trespass and undermine your own life? Is revenge sweeter than immortal life? Indeed is being clever and manipulative sweeter than being healed and perfect and clear of mind? Is that more important? It seems so. I tell you, my beloved people, there is no man or woman that walks the face of the earth, I don't care who they are, that should be worth you losing your dignity, your honor, and your power over. What I mean is that no one should be worth your condemnation, no one should be worth your temptation to manipulate, no one should be worth your need to bear false witness against, and no one should be so important as to undermine them, jeopardizing your own life and your own good fortune because when you do, your soul yells. It is painful. It is a sorrow that can never be bought and all the fame in the world can never relieve. All the men and women in the world will never be able to take it away from you. It is a pain that not even death can quench because it will be carried with you onto the Plane of Bliss.

There are many of you that don't feel worthy of what you are focusing on and you don't feel joy because you don't feel like you are worthy to get it. The problem is that you have a heavy conscience and all of it has to do with some small or large thing, however you see it, that you have created to harm or impede another person's life. When you can stop playing your games and just look at it, and ask your God to forgive you and send you the runner of forgiveness, you will know when that errand has been done because you will feel an incredible lightness of being. And in that comes a joy that has removed such sorrow and such heaviness from your conscience as to be enough of a manifestation. It is a liberator. Then you are back in your divinity. Give and never take. Be honorable and never dishonest. Be truthful, not clever. Be evenly and simply what you are in the depths of your being. You are not evil in your being. No entity was ever created evil because they were created from the Void. That is not evil. There is no such thing. At the core of your being lies divinity. When you have relieved yourself of these burdens through your own simple confession, you will find then that nothing stands in the way of the righteousness and the fruit of your Holy Spirit. It will flow to you in unlimited measure because you are worthy of it. So be it.

No one is a big bad terrible entity but it does feel like it. You think about that. Perhaps when doing your List you can beseech your Holy Spirit to give you clarity on what lies heavy on your soul — ask, you will get it — and then ask to gain the wisdom of your error. When you do, you will know it. Then you are free. Along the path, these are the things that everyone learns. It is the flaws in our life that give us wisdom. Remember that.

WHEN I BECAME THAT CRIMSON FLOWER

In my life I took no elixir — none. I was intoxicated with the Unknown God. In the beginning it was my enemy, the creator of humanity. In the end it was my true love, the giver of life, including me. It was central to my focus. As is common with men and women, enemies are always closer than the ones they profess to love. One loves their enemies more than their dear ones because the enemies occupy more focus, more effort, and more consideration than supposedly those that you say you love. Is that not a wise and logical statement? Here my enemy began as God, the Unknown God, my people's ridiculous entity that allowed their land to go under, allowed greatness to perish, and allowed the wretched aspect of humanity to reign. If the Unknown God so loved these righteous people of my heritage, why then did they and indeed their great and wonderful abilities perish for the sake and in the face of technology? This comes closer to you when those that are closest to you are destroyed, the mother who has issued forth your life as the fruit of her womb and siblings who share with you a genetic imprint.

As a little boy I hated the Unknown God, the lords of the vault of heaven and earth, with such a wrath. There is no power like a child's power, because it is uncorrupted, is focused without logic, and that was my legacy. It was a blessed legacy because God was my enemy and was central to everything that I did. It overrode any sort of social life that today you fight so vigorously to hold onto. There was no social life in my life. This character, this enigma, occupied the mind of the Ram all of its life until the day I left this place.

What was wretched in the beginning became the most precious to me. When I was expanded beyond my genetics and my knowledge, I became that crimson flower on that thorny, insignificant bramble that housed a beautiful songbird. I was caught up in that bird's melody at night, the wonderful care of its children during the day, and the companion of the brambling bush in its ugliness and creepiness only to surprise me with perfumed intoxication and the melody of the bird. It was only when I dared to accept them into my world and into my mind that I then became them, understood their mystery, understood what symbiotic relationship they had here and what really held them together: the crimson flower, the bush and the bird, its melody and perfume, and me sitting there beside them.

It was through such small experiences that caught me up totally and utterly. They allowed me to escape the prison of my hatred, my prejudice, and allowed me to escape into a much milder climate, a much milder consciousness. When I did, I understood women going down to the river, pulling up their long skirts, washing their linen, or weaving that fine linen under water, or bathing their babes. It wasn't until I could be life that I could understand it. In understanding and being it, I understood God, the Unknown God, a faceless entity, only to be caught in a million glimmers of saffron dust, the high note of a beautiful bird, and the deep throat of a crimson flower. That is where I finally found it and found myself in the midst of it.

I did not need to ingest anything to be what I became because I didn't need anything to align my focus. It was already aligned for me. I didn't go off the beaten path and become a fanatic. I didn't go off my beaten path. I didn't do any of that. I enjoyed the unfolding. No one told me I had to do this because I had no teacher that taught me these things, only life. What this proves to you, and perhaps inspires you who don't have a central focus and are struggling to get one, is that perhaps the only enemy you ever had was yourself, but that enemy gets caught up in a hundred reflections from your family, your loves, your hates, your likes and dislikes, your comparisons, your food, your wine, your drug-addiction abuse. You see, you are scattered. The enemy is everywhere because the enemy is you, and you don't have the dynamics that I came into in my life. You haven't been blessed to have a hell of a life. You haven't been blessed to live in a time of world chaos. You haven't been blessed to live in a time of famine, the earth falling out from under you, fabulous cities crumbling overnight, and tyranny rising up all around you. You haven't come from that kind of fire. You came from a very different fire, one that has lulled you into sleep, into your comfort, and the need for your recognition. People only become famous because they need to be recognized. Whether that fame is worldwide or in your family or in your neighborhood, it is a great indicator of a sickness, a great sickness.

You come here fighting an enemy that is yourself, because you are so ignorant. When you have gradually faced the enemy within you, then you come to a singular focus. This is what the school is about. This is the conquest of this journey and this enemy. It takes a lot to get you just to focus on what is the miraculous in your life. It takes a lot to pull you away from your sicknesses. It takes a lot to reason you away from arguing for your limitations. It takes a lot of effort. If you were singularly focused beings, we wouldn't have this. We would already be well on our way.

In my life I was in ecstasy for the Unknown God because I had felt it in everything, and at the end of my life I utterly embodied it. I can tell you straightaway that I, as Ramtha, became enlightened because I was never a hypocrite to myself — never. I never intellectualized why I was a conqueror, a murderer, why I should have the broadsword, why I should conquer. I just did it because it was the process from the central part of my focus, a hatred for life. That was enough. I didn't have to be psychoanalyzed to find out the root cause. I knew it. When my transformation came, I didn't have to do anything because I had already faced the enemy. And because I hadn't made up so many fantasies about myself and told so many stories about myself that were lies — I never did that — I never had anything to work through. So I was clear and embodied it. No one told me that I couldn't. No one told me this was impossible, nor did I ask them if it were. Am I going to ask my generals is it impossible to be the wind? I may have been a simple barbarian but I understood that you don't ask about the marvels of the unknown to fat old men, because if they knew it they wouldn't be fat old men. It is very simple. I never asked. I just was it.

What I have taught you is that every single one of you can be transformed. You can go all the way home, and all the way home is the flowering of God in humanity. That is what Christ is about. You are your savior. The very creature you are trying to run away from is the very creature that is going to bring you back into the bosom of God. The one who you have to catch and save is yourself.

Among everything that you have found important, perhaps the most wonderful thing you should realize is that you are your own enemy. This should be the greatest teaching of all because then we have to look no further. We find it within, and you have been well-equipped on how to defeat lack, insecurity, hatred. You have been taught how to defeat the guilty conscience that you bear, the iniquities that you bear. You have been taught how to defeat all of these things. In the end you have been given the tool for conquering yourself, and that is all you need to do. For many of you that is a terrible battle because it has served you so well to be victims. It has. Your habits have served you so well because you like to get in people's faces and say, "This is the way that I am." Well, don't you get in my face and say that because I know that is not the way you are. It has served you to be complex. It has served you to be stupid. It has served you to be your image. It has served you to suffer because in suffering you make other people suffer. It has served you to be hateful and resentful, but on the other hand it has also served you to be loving and forgiving. It has served you to have concern, and it has served you to have passion for the Great Work. You don't have to look out there anymore. The enemy is not out there. It is inside of you, as well as your savior is inside of you.

If you ask the psychiatrist and parapsychiatrist whether this is right, they will say that I am stressing the minds of its citizenry and telling you about impossible things that can't be accomplished. You must also understand that the only people they have been studying are the villagers who were left behind. The masters are those who have gone beyond. I certainly hope that you just didn't let me talk to you while you were dreamy-eyed. I would certainly desire that what I have said to you has moved you to a new understanding and has given you the liberty and freedom to change your life and make that change the most important thing in your life. Apply what I have taught you. It works.

God bless your life.
So be it.

— *Ramtha*

EPILOGUE BY JZ KNIGHT: HOW IT ALL STARTED

*"In other words, his whole point of focus is to come here
and to teach you to be extraordinary."*

My name is JZ Knight and I am the rightful owner of
this body. Ramtha and I are two different people, two
different beings. We have a common reality point and
that is usually my body. Though we sort of look the same,
we really don't look the same.

All of my life, ever since I was a little person, I have
heard voices in my head and I have seen wonderful things
that to me in my life were normal. I was fortunate enough
to have a mother who was a very psychic human being
and never condemned what it was that I was seeing. I had
wonderful experiences all my life but the most important
experience was that I had this deep and profound love for
God and there was a part of me that understood what that
was. Later in my life I went to church and I tried to
understand God from the viewpoint of religious doctrine
and had a lot of difficulty with that because it was sort of
in conflict with what I felt and what I knew.

Ramtha has been a part of my life ever since I was
born, but I didn't know who he was and I didn't know
what he was, only that there was a wonderful force that
walked with me, and when I was in trouble — and I had a
lot of pain in my life growing up — that I always had
extraordinary experiences with this being who would talk
to me. I could hear him as clearly as I can hear you if we
were to have a conversation. He helped me to understand
a lot of things in my life that were beyond the normal

scope of what someone would give someone as advice.

It wasn't until 1977 that he appeared to me in my kitchen on a Sunday afternoon as I was making pyramids with my husband. We were dehydrating food because we were into hiking and backpacking. As I put one of these ridiculous things on my head, at the other end of my kitchen this wonderful apparition appeared that was seven feet tall and glittery and beautiful and stark. You just don't expect at 2:30 in the afternoon that this is going to appear in your kitchen. No one is ever prepared for that. So Ramtha at that time really made his appearance known to me.

The first thing I said to him — and I don't know where this came from — was, "You are so beautiful. Who are you?" He has a smile like the sun. He is extraordinarily handsome. He said, "My name is Ramtha the Enlightened One and I have come to help you over the ditch." Being the simple person that I am, my immediate reaction was to look at the floor because I thought maybe something had happened to the floor, or the bomb was being dropped. I didn't know. From that day forward he became a constant in my life. And during the year of 1977 a lot of interesting things happened, to say the least. My two younger children at that time got to meet Ramtha and got to experience some incredible phenomena, as well as my husband.

Later that year, after teaching me and having some difficulty telling me what he was and me understanding, one day he said to me, "I am going to send you a runner that will bring you a set of books, and you read them because then you will know what I am." Those books were called the *Life and Teaching of the Masters of the Far East* (DeVorss & Co. Publishers, 1964). I read them and I began to understand that Ramtha was one of those beings, in a way, and that took me out of the are-you-the-devil-or-are-you-God sort of category that was plaguing me at the time.

After I got to understand him he spent long, long moments walking into my living room, all seven feet of this beautiful being, making himself comfortable on my couch, sitting down and talking to me and teaching me. What I didn't realize at that particular time was he already knew all the things I was going to ask and he already knew how to answer them, but I didn't know that he knew that.

Since 1977 he patiently dealt with me in a manner that allowed me to question not his authenticity but things about myself as God, teaching me, catching me when I would get caught up in dogma or get caught up in limitation, catching me just in time and teaching me and walking me through that. And I always said, "You know, you are so patient. I think it is wonderful that you are so patient." And he would just smile and say that he is 35,000 years old, what else can you do in that period of time? It wasn't until about ten years ago that I realized that he already knew what I was going to ask and that is why he was so patient. But as the grand teacher that he is, he allowed me the opportunity to address these issues in myself. He had the grace to speak to me in a way that was not presumptuous but, as a true teacher, would allow me to come to realizations on my own.

Channeling Ramtha since late 1979 has been an experience. Ram is seven feet tall and he wears two robes that I have always seen him in. Even though they are the same robe, they are really beautiful so you never get tired of seeing them. The inner robe is snow white and goes all the way down to where I presume his feet are, and then he has an overrobe that is beautiful purple. You should understand that I have really looked at the material on these robes and it is not really material; it is sort of like light. And though the light has a transparency to them, there is an understanding that what he is wearing has a reality to it.

Ramtha's face is cinnamon-colored skin, and that is the best way I can describe it. It is not really brown and it is not really white and it is not really red. It is sort of a blending of that. He has very deep black eyes that can look into you, and you know you are being looked into. He has eyebrows that look like wings of a bird that come high on his brow. He has a very square jaw and a beautiful mouth, and when he smiles you know that you are in heaven. He has long, long hands and long fingers that he uses very eloquently to demonstrate his thought.

Imagine then after he taught me to get out of my body by actually pulling me out, throwing me in the tunnel, hitting the wall of light and bouncing back — and realizing my kids were home from school and I just got through doing breakfast dishes — that getting used to missing time on this plane was really difficult. I didn't understand what I was doing and where I was going, so we had a lot of practice sessions. You have to understand that he did this to me at ten o'clock in the morning and when I came back off of the white wall it was 4:30. I had a real problem trying to adjust with the time that was missing here. So we had a long time with Ramtha teaching me how to do that, and it was fun and frolic and absolutely terrifying at moments. You can imagine if he walked up to you, yanked you right out of your body, threw you up to the ceiling and said, "Now what does that view look like?" and then throwing you in a tunnel — and perhaps the best way to describe it is it is a black hole into the next level — and being flung through this tunnel and hitting this white wall and having amnesia.

What he was getting me ready to do was to teach me something that I had already agreed to prior to this incarnation. My destiny in this life was not just to marry and to have children and to do well in life but to overcome the adversity to let what was previously planned happen, and that happening included an extraordinary consciousness, which he is.

Trying to dress my body for Ramtha was a joke. I didn't know what to do. The first time we had a channeling session I wore heels and a skirt. I thought I was going to church. So you can imagine, if you have a little time to study him, how he would appear dressed up in a business suit with heels on, which he never walked in in his life.

It is really difficult to talk to people and have them understand that I am not him, that we are two separate beings and that when you talk to me in this body, you are talking to me and not him. Sometimes over the past decade or so, that has been a great challenge to me in the public media because people don't understand how it is possible that a human being can be endowed with a divine mind and yet be separate from it.

I wanted you to know that although you see Ramtha out here in my body, it is my body, but he doesn't look anything like this. His appearance in the body doesn't lessen the magnitude of who and what he is. You should also know that when we do talk, when you start asking me about things that he said, I may not have a clue what you are talking about because when I leave my body, I am gone to a whole other time and another place that I don't have cognizant memory of. And however long he spends with you, to me that will be maybe about five minutes or three minutes. And when I come back to my body, this whole time of this whole day has passed and I wasn't a part of it. I didn't hear what he said to you and I don't know what he did out here. When I come back, my body is exhausted. It is hard to get up the stairs sometimes to change my clothes and make myself more presentable for what the day is bringing me, or what is left of the day.

He has shown me a lot of wonderful things that I suppose people who have never gotten to see couldn't even dream of in their wildest dreams. I have seen the twenty-third universe and I have met extraordinary beings and I have seen life come and go. I have watched generations be born and live and pass in a matter of moments. I have been exposed to historical events to help me understand better what it was I needed to know. I have been allowed to walk beside my body in other lifetimes and watch how I was and who I was, and I have been allowed to see the other side of death. These are cherished and privileged opportunities that somewhere in my life I earned the right to have them. To speak of them to other people is, in a way, disenchanting because it is difficult to convey to people who have never been to those places what it is. I try my best as a storyteller to tell them and still fall short of it.

I also know that the reason that he works with his students the way that he does is because Ramtha never wants to overshadow any of you. In other words, his whole point of focus is to come here and to teach you to be extraordinary. He already is. And it is not about him producing phenomena. If he told you he was going to send you runners, you are going to get them big time. It is not about him doing tricks in front of you. That is not what he is. Those are tools of an avatar that is still a guru that needs to be worshiped, and that is not the case with him.

So what will happen is he will teach you and cultivate you and allow you to create the phenomenon, and you will be able to do that. Then one day when you are able to manifest on cue and you are able to leave your body and you are able to love, when it is to the human interest impossible to do that, he will walk right out here in your life because you are ready to share what he is. And what he is is simply what you are going to become. Until then he is diligent, patient, all-knowing, and all-understanding of everything that we need to know in order to learn to be that.

The one thing I can say to you is that if you are interested in his presentation, and you are starting to love him even though you can't see him, that is a good sign because it means that what was important in you was your soul urging you to unfold in this lifetime. And it may be against your neuronet. Your personality can argue with you and debate with you, but that sort of logic is really transparent when the soul urges you onto an experience.

If this is what you want to do, you are going to have to exercise patience and focus and you are going to have to do the work. The work in the beginning is very hard, but if you have the tenacity to stay with it, then one day I can tell you that this teacher is going to turn you inside out. One day you will be able to do all the remarkable things that you have heard the masters in myth and legend have the capacity to do. You will be able to do them because that is the journey. And ultimately that ability is singularly the reality of a God awakening in human form.

Now that is my journey and it has been my journey all of my life. If it wasn't important and if it wasn't what it was, I certainly wouldn't be living in oblivion most of the year for the sake of having a few people come to have a New Age experience. This is far greater than a New Age experience. I should also say that it is far more important than the ability to meditate or the ability to do yoga. It is about changing consciousness all through our lives on every point and to be able to unhinge and unlimit our minds so that we can be all we can be.

You should also know what I have learned is that we can only demonstrate what we are capable of demonstrating. If you would say, well, what is blocking me from doing that, the only block that we have is our inability to surrender, to allow, and to support ourself even in the face of our own neuronet of doubt. If you can support yourself through doubt, then you will make the breakthrough because that is the only block that stands in your way. And one day you are going to do all these things and get to see all the things that I have seen and been allowed to see.

So I just wanted to come out here and show you that I exist, that I love what I do, and that I hope that you are learning from this teacher. And, more importantly, I hope you continue with it.

— *JZ Knight*

Ramtha's Glossary

Analogical. Being analogical means living in the Now. It is the creative moment and is outside of time, the past, and the emotions.

Analogical mind. Analogical mind means one mind. It is the result of the alignment of primary consciousness and secondary consciousness, the Observer and the personality. The fourth, fifth, sixth, and seventh seals of the body are opened in this state of mind. The bands spin in opposite directions, like a wheel within a wheel, creating a powerful vortex that allows the thoughts held in the frontal lobe to coagulate and manifest.

Bands, the. The bands are the two sets of seven frequencies that surround the human body and hold it together. Each of the seven frequency layers of each band corresponds to the seven seals of seven levels of consciousness in the human body. The bands are the auric field that allow the processes of binary and analogical mind.

Binary mind. This term means two minds. It is the mind produced by accessing the knowledge of the human personality and the physical body without accessing our deep subconscious mind. Binary mind relies solely on the knowledge, perception, and thought processes of the neocortex and the first three seals. The fourth, fifth, sixth, and seventh seals remain closed in this state of mind.

Blue Body®. It is the body that belongs to the fourth plane of existence, the bridge consciousness, and the ultraviolet frequency band. The Blue Body® is the lord over the lightbody and the physical plane.

Blue Body® Dance. It is a discipline taught by Ramtha in which the students lift their conscious awareness to the consciousness of the fourth plane. This discipline allows the Blue Body® to be accessed and the fourth seal to be opened.

Blue Body® Healing. It is a discipline taught by Ramtha in which the students lift their conscious awareness to the consciousness of the fourth plane and the Blue Body® for the purpose of healing or changing the physical body.

Blue webs. The blue webs represent the basic structure at a subtle level of the physical body. It is the invisible skeletal structure of the physical realm vibrating at the level of ultraviolet frequency.

Body/mind consciousness. The consciousness that belongs to the physical plane and the human body.

Book of Life. Ramtha refers to the soul as the Book of Life, where the whole journey of involution and evolution of each individual is recorded in the form of wisdom.

C&E® = R. Consciousness and energy create the nature of reality.

C&E®. Abbreviation of Consciousness & Energy℠. This is the service mark of the fundamental discipline of manifestation and the raising of consciousness taught in Ramtha's School of Enlightenment. Through this discipline the students learn to create an analogical state of mind, open up their higher seals, and create reality from the Void. A Beginning Retreat is the name of the Introductory C&E® event for beginning students in which they learn the fundamental concepts and disciplines of Ramtha's teachings. The introductory teachings can be found in *Ramtha, A Beginner's Guide to Creating Reality,* third ed. (Yelm: JZK Publishing, a division of JZK, Inc., 2004). Students who wish to learn the techniques and disciplines created by Ramtha can receive this instruction personally by participating in one of the events offered by Ramtha's School.

Christwalk. The Christwalk is a discipline designed by Ramtha in which the student learns to walk very slowly being acutely aware. In this discipline the students learn to manifest, with each step they take, the mind of a Christ.

Consciousness. Consciousness is the child who was born from the Void's contemplation of itself. It is the essence and fabric of all being. Everything that exists originated in consciousness and manifested outwardly through its handmaiden energy. A stream of consciousness refers to the continuum of the mind of God.

Consciousness and energy. Consciousness and energy are the dynamic force of creation and are inextricably combined. Everything that exists originated in consciousness and manifested through the modulation of its energy impact into mass.

Create Your Day℠. This is the service mark for a technique created by Ramtha for raising consciousness and energy and intentionally creating a constructive plan of experiences and events for the day early in the morning before the start of the day. This technique is exclusively taught at Ramtha's School of Enlightenment.

Disciplines of the Great Work. Ramtha's School of Ancient Wisdom is dedicated to the Great Work. The disciplines of the Great Work practiced in Ramtha's School of Enlightenment are all designed in their entirety by Ramtha. These practices are powerful initiations where the student has the opportunity to apply and experience firsthand the teachings of Ramtha.

Emotional body. The emotional body is the collection of past emotions, attitudes, and electrochemical patterns that make up the brain's neuronet and define the human personality of an individual. Ramtha describes it as the seduction of the unenlightened. It is the reason for cyclical reincarnation.

Emotions. An emotion is the physical, biochemical effect of an experience. Emotions belong to the past, for they are the expression of experiences that are already known and mapped in the neuropathways of the brain.

Energy. Energy is the counterpart of consciousness. All consciousness carries with it a dynamic energy impact, radiation, or natural expression of itself. Likewise, all forms of energy carry with it a consciousness that defines it.

Enlightenment. Enlightenment is the full realization of the human person, the attainment of immortality, and unlimited mind. It is the result of raising the kundalini energy sitting at the base of the spine to the seventh seal that opens the dormant parts of the brain. When the energy penetrates the lower cerebellum and the midbrain, and the subconscious mind is opened, the individual experiences a blinding flash of light called enlightenment.

Evolution. Evolution is the journey back home from the slowest levels of frequency and mass to the highest levels of consciousness and Point Zero.

Fieldwork^SM. Fieldwork^SM is one of the fundamental disciplines of Ramtha's School of Enlightenment. The students are taught to create a symbol of something they want to know and experience and draw it on a paper card. These cards are placed with the blank side facing out on the fence rails of a large field. The students blindfold themselves and focus on their symbol, allowing their body to walk freely to find their card through the application of the law of consciousness and energy and analogical mind.

Fifth plane. The fifth plane of existence is the plane of superconsciousness and x-ray frequency. It is also known as the Golden Plane or paradise.

Fifth seal. This seal is the center of our spiritual body that connects us to the fifth plane. It is associated with the thyroid gland and with speaking and living the truth without dualism.

First plane. It refers to the material or physical plane. It is the plane of the image consciousness and Hertzian frequency. It is the slowest and densest form of coagulated consciousness and energy.

First seal. The first seal is associated with the reproductive organs, sexuality, and survival.

First three seals. The first three seals are the seals of sexuality, pain and suffering, and controlling power. These are the seals commonly at play in all of the complexities of the human drama.

Fourth plane. The fourth plane of existence is the realm of the bridge consciousness and ultraviolet frequency. This plane is described as the plane of Shiva, the destroyer of the old and creator of the new. In this plane, energy is not yet split into positive and negative polarity. Any lasting changes or healing of the physical body must be changed first at the level of the fourth plane and the Blue Body®. This plane is also called the Blue Plane, or the plane of Shiva.

Fourth seal. The fourth seal is associated with unconditional love and the thymus gland. When this seal is activated, a hormone is released that maintains the body in perfect health and stops the aging process.

God. Ramtha's teachings are an exposition of the statement, "You are God." Humanity is described as the forgotten Gods, divine beings by nature who have forgotten their heritage and true identity. It is precisely this statement that represents Ramtha's challenging message to our modern age, an age riddled with religious superstition and misconceptions about the divine and the true knowledge of wisdom.

God within. It is the Observer, the great self, the primary consciousness, the Spirit, the God within the human person.

God/man. The full realization of a human being.

God/woman. The full realization of a human being.

Gods. The Gods are technologically advanced beings from other star systems who came to Earth 455,000 years ago. These Gods manipulated the human race genetically, mixing and modifying our DNA with theirs. They are responsible for the evolution of the neocortex and used the human race as a subdued work force. Evidence of these events is recorded in the Sumerian tablets and artifacts. This term is also used to describe the true identity of humanity, the forgotten Gods.

Golden body. It is the body that belongs to the fifth plane, superconsciousness, and x-ray frequency.

Great Work. The Great Work is the practical application of the knowledge of the Schools of Ancient Wisdom. It refers to the disciplines by which the human person becomes enlightened and is transmuted into an immortal, divine being.

Grid^SM, The. This is the service mark for a technique created by Ramtha for raising consciousness and energy and intentionally tapping into the field of Zero Point Energy and the fabric of reality through a mental visualization. This technique is exclusively taught at Ramtha's School of Enlightenment.

Hierophant. A hierophant is a master teacher who is able to manifest what they teach and initiate their students into such knowledge.

Hyperconsciousness. Hyperconsciousness is the consciousness of the sixth plane and gamma ray frequency.

Infinite Unknown. It is the frequency band of the seventh plane of existence and ultraconsciousness.

Involution. Involution is the journey from Point Zero and the seventh plane to the slowest and densest levels of frequency and mass.

JZ Knight. JZ Knight is the only person appointed by Ramtha to channel him. Ramtha refers to JZ as his beloved daughter. She was Ramaya, the eldest of the children given to Ramtha during his lifetime.

Kundalini. Kundalini energy is the life force of a person that descends from the higher seals to the base of the spine at puberty. It is a large packet of energy reserved for human evolution, commonly pictured as a coiled serpent that sits at the base of the spine. This energy is different from the energy coming out of the first three seals responsible for sexuality, pain and suffering, power, and victimization. It is commonly described as the sleeping serpent or the sleeping dragon. The journey of the kundalini energy to the crown of the head is called the journey of enlightenment. This journey takes place when this serpent wakes up and starts to split and dance around the spine, ionizing the spinal fluid and changing its molecular structure. This action causes the opening of the midbrain and the door to the subconscious mind.

Life review. It is the review of the previous incarnation that occurs when the person reaches the third plane after death. The person gets the opportunity to be the Observer, the actor, and the recipient of its own actions. The unresolved issues from that lifetime that emerge at the life or light review set the agenda for the next incarnation.

Light, the. The light refers to the third plane of existence.

Lightbody. It is the same as the radiant body. It is the body that belongs to the third plane of conscious awareness and the visible light frequency band.

List, the. The List is the discipline taught by Ramtha where the student gets to write a list of items they desire to know and experience and then learn to focus on it in an analogical state of consciousness. The List is the map used to design, change, and reprogram the neuronet of the person. It is the tool that helps to bring meaningful and lasting changes in the person and their reality.

Make known the unknown. This phrase expresses the original divine mandate given to the Source consciousness to manifest and bring to conscious awareness all of the infinite potentials of the Void. This statement represents the basic intent that inspires the dynamic process of creation and evolution.

Mind. Mind is the product of streams of consciousness and energy acting on the brain creating thought-forms, holographic segments, or neurosynaptic patterns called memory. The streams of consciousness and energy are what keep the brain alive. They are its power source. A person's ability to think is what gives them a mind.

Mind of God. The mind of God comprises the mind and wisdom of every lifeform that ever lived on any dimension, in any time, or that ever will live on any planet, any star, or region of space.

Mirror consciousness. When Point Zero imitated the act of contemplation of the Void it created a mirror reflection of itself, a point of reference that made the exploration of the Void possible. It is called mirror consciousness or secondary consciousness. See **Self.**

Monkey-mind. Monkey-mind refers to the flickering, swinging mind of the personality.

Mother/Father Principle. It is the source of all life, the Father, the eternal Mother, the Void. In Ramtha's teachings, the Source and God the creator are not the same. God the creator is seen as Point Zero and primary consciousness but not as the Source, or the Void, itself.

Name-field. The name-field is the name of the large field where the discipline of Fieldwork^{SM} is practiced.

Neighborhood Walk^{SM}. This is the service mark of a technique created by JZ Knight for raising consciousness and energy and intentionally modifying our neuronets and set patterns of thinking no longer wanted and replacing them with new ones of our choice. This technique is exclusively taught at Ramtha's School of Enlightenment.

Neuronet. The contraction for "neural network," a network of neurons that perform a function together.

Observer. It refers to the Observer responsible for collapsing the particle/wave of quantum mechanics. It represents the great self, the Spirit, primary consciousness, the God within the human person.

Outrageous. Ramtha uses this word in a positive way to express something or someone who is extraordinary and unusual, unrestrained in action, and excessively bold or fierce.

People, places, things, times, and events. These are the main areas of human experience to which the personality is emotionally attached. These areas represent the past of the human person and constitute the content of the emotional body.

Personality, the. *See* **Emotional body.**

Plane of Bliss. It refers to the plane of rest where souls get to plan their next incarnations after their life reviews. It is also known as heaven and paradise where there is no suffering, no pain, no need or lack, and where every wish is immediately manifested.

Plane of demonstration. The physical plane is also called the plane of demonstration. It is the plane where the person has the opportunity to demonstrate its creative potentiality in mass and witness consciousness in material form in order to expand its emotional understanding.

Point Zero. It refers to the original point of awareness created by the Void through its act of contemplating itself. Point Zero is the original child of the Void, the birth of consciousness.

Primary consciousness. It is the Observer, the great self, the God within the human person.

Ram. Ram is a shorter version of the name Ramtha. Ramtha means the Father.

Ramaya. Ramtha refers to JZ Knight as his beloved daughter. She was Ramaya, the first one to become Ramtha's adopted child during his lifetime. Ramtha found Ramaya abandoned on the steppes of Russia. Many people gave their children to Ramtha during the march as a gesture of love and highest respect; these children were to be raised in the House of the Ram. His children grew to the great number of 133 even though he never had offspring of his own blood.

Ramtha (etymology). The name of Ramtha the Enlightened One, Lord of the Wind, means the Father. It also refers to the Ram who descended from the mountain on what is known as the terrible day of the Ram. "It is about that in all antiquity. And in ancient Egypt, there is an avenue dedicated to the Ram, the great conqueror. And they were wise enough to understand that whoever could walk down the avenue of the Ram could conquer the wind." The word Aram, the name of Noah's grandson, is formed from the Aramaic noun Araa — meaning earth, landmass — and the word Ramtha, meaning high. This Semitic name echoes Ramtha's descent from the high mountain, which began the great march.

Runner. A runner in Ramtha's lifetime was responsible for bringing specific messages or information. A master teacher has the ability to send runners to other people that manifest their words or intent in the form of an experience or an event.

Second plane. It is the plane of existence of social consciousness and the infrared frequency band. It is associated with pain and suffering. This plane is the negative polarity of the third plane of visible light frequency.

Second seal. This seal is the energy center of social consciousness and the infrared frequency band. It is associated with the experience of pain and suffering and is located in the lower abdominal area.

Secondary consciousness. When Point Zero imitated the act of contemplation of the Void it created a mirror reflection of itself, a point of reference that made the exploration of the Void possible. It is called mirror consciousness or secondary consciousness. *See* **Self.**

Self, the. The self is the true identity of the human person different from the personality. It is the transcendental aspect of the person. It refers to the secondary consciousness, the traveler in a journey of involution and evolution making known the unknown.

Sending-and-receiving. Sending-and-receiving is the name of the discipline taught by Ramtha in which the student learns to access information using the faculties of the midbrain to the exclusion of sensory perception.

Seven seals. The seven seals are powerful energy centers that constitute seven levels of consciousness in the human body. The bands are the way in which the physical body is held together according to these seals. In every human being there is energy spiraling out of the first three seals or centers. The energy pulsating out of the first three seals manifests itself respectively as sexuality, pain, or power. When the upper seals are unlocked, a higher level of awareness is activated.

Seventh plane. The seventh plane is the plane of ultraconsciousness and the Infinite Unknown frequency band. This plane is where the journey of involution began. This plane was created by Point Zero when it imitated the act of contemplation of the Void and the mirror or secondary consciousness was created. A plane of existence or dimension of space and time exists between two points of consciousness. All the other planes were created by slowing down the time and frequency band of the seventh plane.

Seventh seal. This seal is associated with the crown of the head, the pituitary gland, and the attainment of enlightenment.

Shiva. The Lord God Shiva represents the Lord of the Blue Plane and the Blue Body®. Shiva is not used in reference to a singular deity from Hinduism. It is rather the representation of a state of consciousness that belongs to the fourth plane, the ultraviolet frequency band, and the opening of the fourth seal. Shiva is neither male nor female. It is an androgynous being, for the energy of the fourth plane has not yet been split into positive and negative polarity. This is an important distinction from the traditional Hindu representation of Shiva as a male deity who has a wife. The tiger skin at its feet, the trident staff, and the sun and the moon at the level of the head represent the mastery of this body over the first three seals of consciousness. The kundalini energy is pictured as fiery energy shooting from the base of the spine through the head. This is another distinction from some Hindu representations of Shiva with the serpent energy coming out at the level of the fifth seal or throat. Another symbolic image of Shiva is the long threads of dark hair and an abundance of pearl necklaces, which represent its richness of experience owned into wisdom. The quiver and bow and arrows are the agent by which Shiva shoots its powerful will and destroys imperfection and creates the new.

Sixth plane. The sixth plane is the realm of hyperconsciousness and the gamma ray frequency band. In this plane the awareness of being one with the whole of life is experienced.

Sixth seal. This seal is associated with the pineal gland and the gamma ray frequency band. The reticular formation that filters and veils the knowingness of the subconscious mind is opened when this seal is activated. The opening of the brain refers to the opening of this seal and the activation of its consciousness and energy.

Social consciousness. It is the consciousness of the second plane and the infrared frequency band. It is also called the image of the human personality and the mind of the first three seals. Social consciousness refers to the collective consciousness of human society. It is the collection of thoughts, assumptions, judgments, prejudices, laws, morality, values, attitudes, ideals, and emotions of the fraternity of the human race.

Soul. Ramtha refers to the soul as the Book of Life, where the whole journey of involution and evolution of the individual is recorded in the form of wisdom.

Subconscious mind. The seat of the subconscious mind is the lower cerebellum or reptilian brain. This part of the brain has its own independent connections to the frontal lobe and the whole of the body and has the power to access the mind of God, the wisdom of the ages.

Superconsciousness. This is the consciousness of the fifth plane and the x-ray frequency band.

Tahumo. Tahumo is the discipline taught by Ramtha in which the student learns the ability to master the effects of the natural environment — cold and heat — on the human body.

Tank field. It is the name of the large field with the labyrinth that is used for the discipline of The Tank®.

Tank®, The. It is the name given to the labyrinth used as part of the disciplines of Ramtha's School of Enlightenment. The students are taught to find the entry to this labyrinth blindfolded and move through it focusing on the Void without touching the walls or using the eyes or the senses. The objective of this discipline is to find, blindfolded, the center of the labyrinth or a room designated and representative of the Void.

Third plane. This is the plane of conscious awareness and the visible light frequency band. It is also known as the light plane and the mental plane. When the energy of the Blue Plane is lowered down to this frequency band, it splits into positive and negative polarity. It is at this point that the soul splits into two, giving origin to the phenomenon of soulmates.

Third seal. This seal is the energy center of conscious awareness and the visible light frequency band. It is associated with control, tyranny, victimization, and power. It is located in the region of the solar plexus.

Thought. Thought is different from consciousness. The brain processes a stream of consciousness, modifying it into segments — holographic pictures — of neurological, electrical, and chemical prints called thoughts. Thoughts are the building blocks of mind.

Torsion Process^{SM}. This is the service mark of a technique created by Ramtha for raising consciousness and energy and intentionally creating a torsion field using the mind. Through this technique the student learns to build a wormhole in space/time, alter reality, and create dimensional phenomena such as invisibility, levitation, bilocation, teleportation, and others. This technique is exclusively taught at Ramtha's School of Enlightenment.

Twilight®. This term is used to describe the discipline taught by Ramtha in which the students learn to put their bodies in a catatonic state similar to deep sleep, yet retaining their conscious awareness.

Ultraconsciousness. It is the consciousness of the seventh plane and the Infinite Unknown frequency band. It is the consciousness of an ascended master.

Unknown God. The Unknown God was the single God of Ramtha's ancestors, the Lemurians. The Unknown God also represents the forgotten divinity and divine origin of the human person.

Void, the. The Void is defined as one vast nothing materially, yet all things potentially. *See* **Mother/Father Principle.**

Yellow brain. The yellow brain is Ramtha's name for the neocortex, the house of analytical and emotional thought. The reason why it is called the yellow brain is because the neocortices were colored yellow in the original two-dimensional, caricature-style drawing Ramtha used for his teaching on the function of the brain and its processes. He explained that the different aspects of the brain in this particular drawing are exaggerated and colorfully highlighted for the sake of study and understanding.

Yeshua ben Joseph. Ramtha refers to Jesus Christ by the name Yeshua ben Joseph, following the Jewish traditions of Jesus' lifetime.

Fig. A: The Seven Seals:
Seven Levels of Consciousness in the Human Body

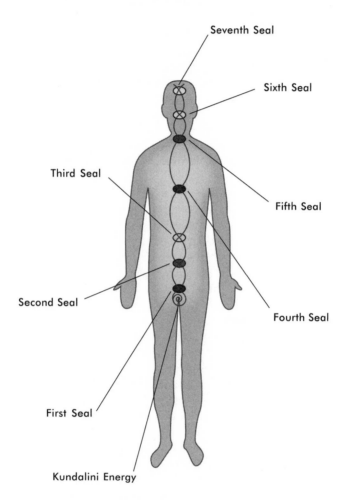

Seventh Seal

Sixth Seal

Third Seal

Fifth Seal

Second Seal

Fourth Seal

First Seal

Kundalini Energy

Fig. B: Seven Levels of Consciousness and Energy

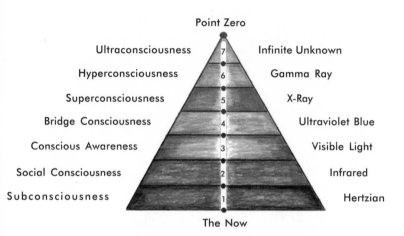

Point Zero

Ultraconsciousness	7	Infinite Unknown
Hyperconsciousness	6	Gamma Ray
Superconsciousness	5	X-Ray
Bridge Consciousness	4	Ultraviolet Blue
Conscious Awareness	3	Visible Light
Social Consciousness	2	Infrared
Subconsciousness	1	Hertzian

The Now

Fig. C: The Brain

Thalamus

Neocortex
(The Yellow Brain)

Hypothalamus

Corpus
Callosum

Frontal Lobe

Midbrain

Pituitary Gland

Pineal
Gland

Hippocampus
and Amygdala

Lower
Cerebellum

Pons

Spinal Cord

Reticular
Formation

Energy

81

Fig. D: Binary Mind — Living the Image

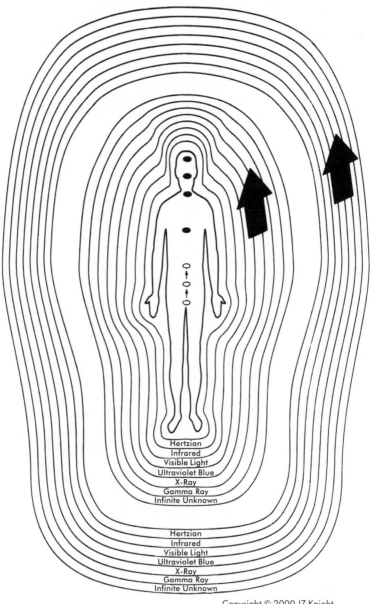

Hertzian
Infrared
Visible Light
Ultraviolet Blue
X-Ray
Gamma Ray
Infinite Unknown

Hertzian
Infrared
Visible Light
Ultraviolet Blue
X-Ray
Gamma Ray
Infinite Unknown

FIG. E: ANALOGICAL MIND — LIVING IN THE NOW

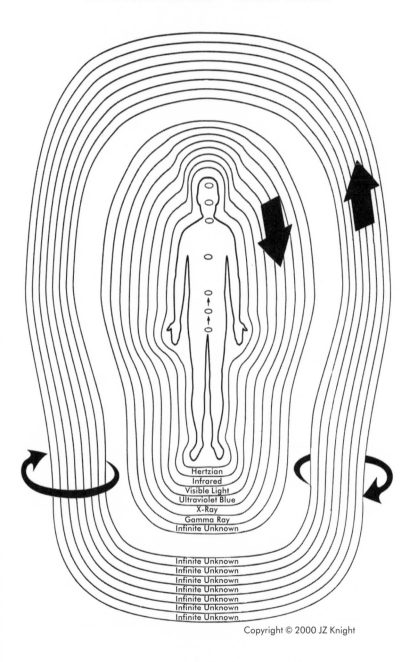

Hertzian
Infrared
Visible Light
Ultraviolet Blue
X-Ray
Gamma Ray
Infinite Unknown

Infinite Unknown
Infinite Unknown
Infinite Unknown
Infinite Unknown
Infinite Unknown
Infinite Unknown
Infinite Unknown

FIG. F: THE OBSERVER EFFECT AND THE NERVE CELL

The Observer is responsible
for collapsing the wave function of probability
into particle reality.

Particle   Energy wave   The Observer

The act of observation
makes the nerve cells fire and produces thought.

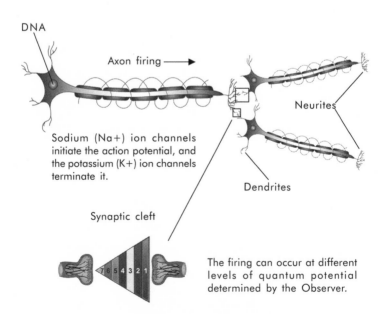

DNA

Axon firing ⟶

Sodium (Na+) ion channels
initiate the action potential, and
the potassium (K+) ion channels
terminate it.

Neurites

Dendrites

Synaptic cleft

The firing can occur at different
levels of quantum potential
determined by the Observer.

Fig. G: Cellular Biology and the Thought Connection

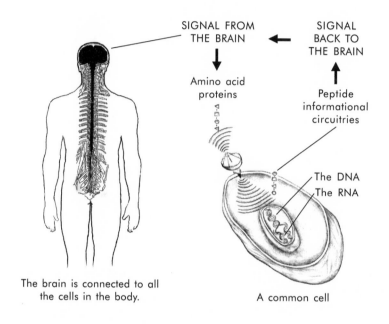

SIGNAL FROM THE BRAIN

SIGNAL BACK TO THE BRAIN

Amino acid proteins

Peptide informational circuitries

The DNA
The RNA

The brain is connected to all the cells in the body.

A common cell

Fig. H: Weblike Skeletal Structure of Mass

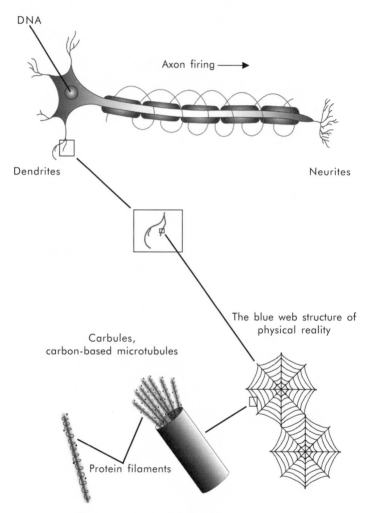

DNA

Axon firing →

Dendrites

Neurites

The blue web structure of physical reality

Carbules, carbon-based microtubules

Protein filaments

Electrons move in and through the protein filaments.

Fig. I: The Blue Body®

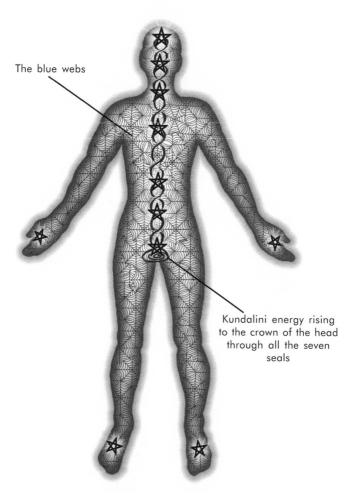

The blue webs

Kundalini energy rising
to the crown of the head
through all the seven
seals

Ramtha's School of Enlightenment
THE SCHOOL OF ANCIENT WISDOM

A Division of JZK, Inc.
P.O. Box 1210
Yelm, Washington 98597
360.458.5201
800.347.0439
www.ramtha.com
www.jzkpublishing.com